Matsuri

T0362813

Shinto Festival

We are going to see the Matsuri parade.

We will see people making the **floats**.

The floats will get bigger and bigger and bigger.

We will see **lanterns** on the floats.

The lanterns are bright.

Look at the men.

The men will pull the floats in the parade.

They are very strong.

We will see the women
in the parade.
The women will wear
beautiful clothes.
They are very happy.

We will see children
with drums in the parade.
They will play the drums.

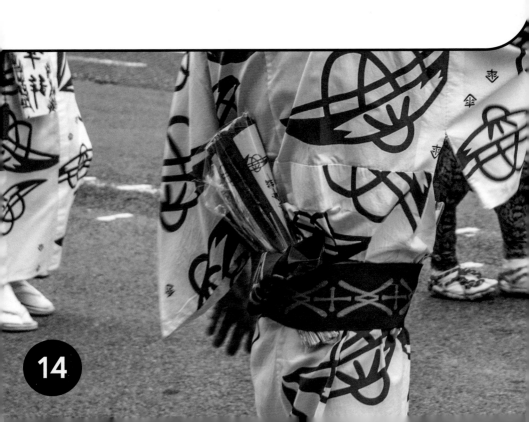

Glossary

floats

lanterns